Myths and Lies Exposed

Satan's Attack on Bible Prophecy News

ERIKA GREY

Pedante Press

Short Book Series

003

DEDICATION

For my father, who made this work possible

CONTENTS

www.erikagrey.com

For Bible Prophecy news and analysis and more books visit my website. For Bible Prophecy Updates on video subscribe to my YouTube channel Prophecy Talk with Erika Grey.

1 DIVISIONS IN THE CHURCH

When it comes to the Gospel, Evangelicals primarily agree on the fundamentals of the faith despite differences in areas. In all other areas there are serious divides among Evangelicals. In these doctrines where they just don't agree. Paul the Apostle spoke against these divisions in 1 Corinthians 1:10. Hel stated, "I appeal to you brothers and sisters, the name of our LORD Jesus Christ, that all of you agree with one another in what you say and that there be no divisions among you, but that you be perfectly united in mind and thought."

Unfortunately, these divisions existed in the early church onto today. Evangelicals emphasize certain doctrines over others and contention exists. From liberal and conservative views, to King James only, disputes over the gifts of the spirit and many more disagreements exist. Paul admonished against divisions and added in I Corinthians 1:12, "Now I say this that each of you says, "I am of Paul' or "I am of Apollos, " or "I am of Cephas" or "I am of Christ". Is Christ divided" Was Paul crucified for you? Or were you baptized in the name of Paul? When we consider all the different denominations under the Evangelical faith umbrella, we see that Christianity has not changed from the days of the apostles.

Disputes Extend to End Time Prophecies

The divisions in the Evangelical community have also entered the realm of the end time prophetic forecasts. For instance, some teach the Rapture and others do not. The Rapture doctrine states that believers in the age of Grace will be taken out of the earth prior to the start of the Tribulation. Theologians call this a pre-tribulation view on the Rapture. Others hold that believers will go through part of the Tribulation. They named this mid-Trib. Others that Jesus only comes once at the second coming. These hold a post-Trib view.

The preterists conclude that part of the prophecies considered end time were already fulfilled. Many of these divisions come down to lack of research in the writings themselves.

2 SOMETHING MORE SINISTER

There is something more sinister happening to end time prophecy. The attack on the teachings extends from the hand of Satan himself. When we enter the realm of Bible Prophecy news, in which Bible Prophecy teachers take not only the prophetic forecasts but current events to provide status updates, out and out lies proliferate. Many Bible Prophecy teachers unknowingly repeat them. In line with the Scripture's warning they teach fables.

How Does the Bible Define Fables?

There are five verses in the New Testament that deal with fables. The word in the Greek used is mythos or myths. It means: a narrative, story, a true narrative, a fiction, a fable, an invention, a falsehood. A tale, that is fiction ("myth") --fable. In other words, a story that is made up.

Paul's Warning Against Those Who Teach Fables

Paul warns about teachings added to the Gospel. In Acts 20:29 he states,

"For I know this, that after my departure savage wolves will come in among you, not sparing the flock. Also, from among yourselves men will rise up, speaking perverse things, to draw away the disciples after themselves. Therefore, watch and remember that for three years I did not cease to warn everyone night and day with tears." While Paul is referring to the Gospel's teachings, his warning applies to prophecy correlations taught in the name of Christ.

In end time prophecy circles, you can get some excellent teachings. But, amidst the truth are the fables and sadly the myths dominate the sound teachings. Paul warned in 1 Timothy 1:4, "Neither give heed to fables and endless genealogies, which minister questions, rather than godly edifying which is in faith: so, do."

2 Timothy Sums It Up Best

The next Bible verse dealing with fables, tells how someone gets hooked on false teachings. 2 Timothy 4:4 reads, "And they shall turn away their ears from the truth and shall be turned unto fables." Part of the reason for this switch is because the lies are enticing. They grip someone's emotions and blind their reasoning.

Peter Names Them "Cunningly Devised Fables"

Peter refers to false teaching that come along the Gospel's message. Cunningly devised fables dominate end time prophecy teacher's reading of the fig tree. The Bible could not have described these lies more perfectly. Many teachers who do not study the Scriptures as the Bible directs repeat these falsehoods. 2 Timothy 2:15 states, "Study to shew thyself approved unto God, a workman that needed not to be ashamed, rightly dividing the world of truth."

In 1 Thessalonians 2:9 we learn that the apostles labored tirelessly day and night. All teachers of Bible Prophecy news should do the same. There is a good deal of study involved. Not only must one master the prophetic forecasts but also world affairs.

We will look at the cunningly devised fables further on. Next we will look at why Satan attacks end time Bible Prophecy more than any other area.

3 JESUS IS THE SPIRIT OF PROPHECY

When one considers the high percentage of fables in end time prophecy news one has to ask why for such an attack. The area of the greatest errors is in the reading of the fig tree. There is a believer I know today who will not follow end time prophecy because he got hooked on false teachings and now refuses to even look at the truth. Many pastor's will not teach on prophecy because they recognize the outlandish and diverse teachings on its unfolding fruition. Satan obviously does not want believers knowing the real status of the fulfillment. Why?

Testimony of Jesus is the Spirit of Prophecy

Satan's attack against end time Bible Prophecy is an attack against Jesus Himself. The Bible tells us the testimony of Jesus is the Spirit of Prophecy. Revelation 19:10 states, "And I fell at his feet to worship him. And He said unto me, See thou do it not: I am thy fellow servant, and of thy brethren that have the testimony of Jesus: worship God: for the testimony of Jesus is the spirit of prophecy."

The Word for Prophecy In the Bible

The word for prophecy in Hebrew means a. discourse emanating from divine inspiration and declaring the purposes of God, whether by reproving and admonishing the wicked, or comforting the afflicted, or revealing things hidden; especially by foretelling future events. Used in the N.T. of utterances of O.T. prophets.

Strong's Concordance Definition of Prophecy

According to *Strong's Concordance*, prophecy tells

future events as they relate to Christ's kingdom and its speedy triumph. Strong's definition for prophecy also includes:

1. prophecy
2. of the prediction of events relating to Christ's kingdom and its speedy triumph, together with the consolations and admonitions pertaining to it, the spirit of prophecy, the divine mind, to which the prophetic faculty is due
3. of the endowment and speech of the Christian teachers called prophets
4. the gifts and utterances of these prophets, esp. of the predictions of the works of which, set apart to teach the gospel, will accomplish for the kingdom of Christ

In conclusion, Bible Prophecy is serious business, which is taken too lightly by those who teach fables and myths.

Jesus's Blessing For those Who He Finds Watching

Jesus promises a blessing for those who when He comes, He finds watching. He promises in Luke 12:37, "Blessed are those servants whom the master, when he comes, will find watching. Assuredly, I say to you that He will gird Himself and have them sit down to eat and will come and serve them. "

This is a major promise. Literally after the Rapture, Jesus has a dinner prepared for those who He found watching for His return.

If you are following fables and myths, will you both miss important details in this watch. In addition, Jesus will not consider you a watcher for following obvious lies.

4 GOD'S QUALIFICATIONS

One of the reasons for the existence of so many cunningly devised fables in end time prophecy news is because no standard exists. Anyone can become a prophecy teacher by having an interest and putting up a website. The Evangelical community's criteria is shallow. Many Evangelicals believe that anyone who is a pastor of a church instantly qualifies. In addition, if a person is from a region in the Middle East and gets converted, they qualify them as well. God clearly set a standard. We find it in His Word as a recurring theme. Christians need to take note. Many who teach do not fit any of the Biblical qualifications.

Prophets Went Before Kings

We see from Scripture that many of the prophets went before Kings. The Old Testament prophets warned rulers during the kingdom period in Israel. Moses went before Pharaoh. Daniel to the Kings of Babylon, and Medo Persia. Joseph went to Pharaoh, Abraham to Abimelek king of Gerar over Sarah

In the New Testament John, the Baptist to Herod, Jesus Himself went before Herod and Caesar. We will look at some of these individuals in more detail.

Special Training-Skills-and Upbringing-Joseph

The Ishmaelites took Joseph to Egypt and sold him into slavery. Potiphar purchased him. According to Genesis 39:1, Potiphar was 'an Egyptian who was one of Pharaoh's officials, the captain of the guard.'"

When Potiphar saw that the Lord was with Joseph, he made him his attendant and then put Joseph in charge of his entire household. God blessed Potiphar and all he had on behalf of Joseph.

While Joseph served Potiphar, he unknowingly was being trained by God to deal with political officials. Working for Potiphar prepared Joseph for going before Pharaoh. No doubt, the time with Potiphar taught Joseph the ways and manner of the 'elite' of his day. Potiphar was one of Pharaoh's cabinet officials. While it was Joseph's gift that brought him before Pharaoh, the time with Potiphar trained him for this meeting. In addition, it also prepared him for the role of Pharaoh's finance minister. Joseph was promoted to second to Pharaoh.

Moses

When Pharaoh decreed to kill all the first-born males of the Israelites, Moses' mother attempted to save her baby boy by building a basket that could float. She then sent Moses afloat in the river. Pharaoh's daughter came across the basket and adopted him. She named him Moses, which means drawn out of water. Thus Moses was raised in a royal family, in Pharaoh's court; with the daughter of Pharaoh as his adopted mother.

Moses's daughter let Moses know of his Jewish roots. This is evidenced by Moses's killing of the Egyptian who beat the Israeli. When Pharaoh ordered the murder of the newborn males, he probably was not happy with his daughter's decision to adopt Moses, but he did not stop her. When Moses murdered the Egyptian, word got to Pharaoh and he then set out to have Moses killed. Moses fled to the wilderness to work as a shepherd. Meanwhile, Pharaoh died, and a new ruler took his place. God called Moses while in Midian.

Moses questioned God why He would choose him to go to Pharaoh and to lead the Israelites out of Egypt. Moses felt inadequate because he was not a speaker and he felt awkward in conversation. While God accommodated Moses, by providing Aaron to speak, Moses possessed something he did not realize.

Moses Upbringing

Moses upbringing was no coincidence. The mother of Moses, she was called on to do what a mother would never expect; give up her child to save it. No doubt she had to trust God in the process. Hebrews 11 noted her faith.

As in the case of Joseph, what someone meant for evil, God used for good. This upbringing was vital for Moses who God would have go to Pharaoh decades later. He was able to speak to him on his terms, in his language. While he felt inadequate because of his speaking capabilities, Moses knew his way around Pharaoh's court. His having been the adopted son of the previous Pharaoh might have gotten him the door for the meeting.

Hebrews 11 commends Moses for going from riches to rags and choosing to be with the people of God rather than have the wealth of Egypt. Moses's and his parent's actions are written in what theologians' regard as the "Hall of Faith." Yet, although Moses forsook his adopted inheritance and the future it could have meant for him, it was a vital stepping stone for the task God had him to do.

The Prophet Daniel

The prophet Daniel was a Babylonian captive. The Babylonians sought out the brightest of the Israeli youth to serve in the Kingdom. They chose Daniel to serve in Nebuchadnezzar's court. The Lord gifted him in all wisdom, knowledge and understanding. So much so that the Antichrist is referenced as having wisdom and knowledge greater than

Daniels. In addition, the Bible tells us Daniel trained for three years in the language and educational system of the Babylonians.

The prophet Daniel held positions of what would today be considered cabinet roles, of a high official. Daniel served in two of the empires that are written about in the book of Daniel. He served under both the Babylonians and the Medes and Persians.

God's method is no different from someone getting saved out of a certain sin, or religion, and are now qualified to go into that area and witness for Christ. We see this in the prophets who God gave specific tasks.

God's Pattern

The pattern becomes evident that when God placed a prophet in a role with a major empire, that prophet had training. Specifically, in dealing with the politicians of the political powers. Thus we see Joseph as Potiphar's assistant and Moses raised as a son of Pharaoh's daughter. In addition, Daniel trained in the Babylonian language and educational system, then onto a role working in Nebuchadnezzar's court.

You might be thinking that this was God's pattern in the Old Testament and does not apply today. While the prophets in the Old Testament were different from the New, we see a similar pattern in the New Testament.

The Magi

At the birth of Jesus there were two prophets. Anna who served in the Temple day and night and John the Baptist: who was an infant at that time. When Herod inquired of the priests and prophets of the king that would be born, he ended up consulting with the magi. These are also known as the wise men. The Bible does not tell us how many there were, or if they were men and women.

These were astronomers and essentially the academics and Biblical Scholars of their day. Their knowledge of the Scriptures was so acute, that their gifts gold, frankincense, and myrrh presented to the young Jesus the completion of the herbal formulations given to Moses. Thus, confirming this was the Christ. This was missed by theologians.

5 STANDARD JESUS ESTABLISHES

Jesus set a standard in Matthew 23:34 when he stated, "Therefore, indeed, I send you prophets, wise men and scribes, some of them you will kill and crucify, and some of them you will scourge in your synagogues and persecute from city to city."

The word for wise men can also include women. In the Old and New Testament, we see wise men as those who consulted Kings. The word has Babylonian origin. It derives from a Magus, meaning teachers, priests, physicians, astrologers, and also included seers, soothsayers and sorcerers. In today's world it would be those we regard as academia, scholars, scientists, business leaders, finance ministers, and cabinet members. This list is not exhaustive but relays the point.

The Apostle John Son of Zebedee

John was the son of Zebedee who was a fisherman of some wealth and means in Capernaum. He owned a fishing enterprise. When Jesus called James and John, they were in the boat mending a net with their father, and his hired help. they left to follow Jesus. When they departed the boat, Zebedee did not protest. Probably for two reasons, as a righteous man he understood the call of God on his son's lives. In addition, he was prosperous and had enough hired help to take on the tasks of his sons.

Zebedee's Name Mentioned Twelve Times

The Bible mention's Zebedee's name is mentioned twelve times. The number represents faith and the church. In two, of the mentions an unusual title is given to Simone the mother of James and John. She is referred to as the mother of Zebedee's children. This is a further elevation of Zebedee. A form of his name in the Old Testament means, "my gift."

What an honor that two of his sons were called to be apostles. Zebedee was blessed by God, both in knowledge of the true God, and was also prosperous in his life.

Sons of Thunder

When Jesus called both James and John the sons of thunder, many misunderstand this to mean that they were rough and explosive, on the contrary, John is the love Apostle. Rather thunder in the Bible is associated with the voice of God and His power. Thus, sons of thunder indicate that each of these would especially receive God's power.

We see this in James who Herod sought out and killed. James became the first martyr. Why did Herod seek out James? He must have stood out in his preaching, for his name to get to Herod. John on the other hand would write not only a Gospel, but three epistles and the book of Revelation. John wrote a considerable portion of the New Testament.

John and the Revelation

In John's upbringing, Zebedee was able to provide him with an education. According to

Scott Michael Rank PHD, editor of History on the Net, in the Roman empire "the only children who received a formal education were the children of the rich. The very rich families employed a private tutor to teach their children. Those that could not afford to do this used either slaves or sent their children to a private school. Children of poor families were not educated at all.

Therefore, Zebedee's wealth most likely allowed John and James an education. In Revelation 1:19 Jesus tells John to "Write the things which you have been and the things which are, and the things which will take place after this."

John and The Early Church Fathers

John wrote of the coming Antichrist and we see John's followers also writing of him. Ignatius and Polycarp were John's disciples. These men wrote of the coming Antichrist and we still have their writings today.

Wise Men Through the Ages

Though the ages we see the wise men that Jesus

sent since giving John the Revelation. From the early church fathers, to Martin Luther. Bible Translators such as Wycliffe. In the area of end time prophecy, we have theologians such as H.A. Ironside 1876-1951. Although he had no formal education, he earned honorary degrees and was dubbed the archbishop of Fundamentalism. He published more than 100 books and pamphlets.

Frank E. Gaebelein, 1899-1983 was a Harvard graduate, Evangelical educator, and author of more than 20 books. He was also the Vice Chairman of Oxford University Press, co-editor of *Christianity Today* in its early days and more.

Arthur. W. Pink, 1886 to 1952, was a pastor and theologian. He briefly attended Moody and in the later part of his life was devoted solely to study and writing. A brilliant man, he wrote excellent pieces on the Antichrist.

John Nelson Darby

John Nelson Darby, 1800-1882, was known as the father of dispensationalism and futurism. He discovered the pretribulation Rapture of the church in Scripture. He was an Anglo-Irish

Bible scholar and teacher, who was also a Bible translator. In addition, he wrote poems and hymns. He was a Brethren who established many churches. He also gave lectures. Darby became known as the leading interpreter of biblical prophecy in his day. In 1829 he predicted the rebirth of the nation of Israel, which occurred 119 years later.

Darby was born into a wealthy family and received the best education available for his era. He was educated at Westminster School and Trinity College, Dublin. He graduated Classical Gold Medalist in 1819, meaning he passed all his exams on the first attempt and achieved the highest marks. Darby began a career in law, he got saved at about 20 years old, according to the Southern California Seminary.

Ian Paisley Jr.

Ian Paisley Jr., 1926 to 2014, was a Protestant evangelical minister, who co-founded the fundamentalist Free Presbyterian Church of Ulster. He became a loyalist politician in Northern Ireland. In his career he sat alongside politicians including former Prime Minister Tony Blair and the Archduke Otto Von

Hapsburg In 1979 to 2004 he served as a member of the EU Parliament. In 1988 during a speech by Pope John Paul II in the EU Parliament, Paisley held up a poster which read, Pope John Paul II ANTICHRIST. He shouted, "I denounce you as the Antichrist." Other MEP's threw papers at him and grabbed his poster, but he produced another.

He was forcibly removed from the chamber. Later he claimed he was injured by other MEP's who struck him and threw objects at him. This included the Archduke Otto Von Hapsburg who later became the subject of conspiracy theorists. Paisley's early writings and website on the European Union provided invaluable insights into the EU in light of end time prophecy.

More on the Wise Men

The above-mentioned wise men are not an exhausted list, but an example. Ironside and Gaebelin wrote on the final world empire. Their observations were spot on when there were no telltale signs other than the EU's initial formation in 1951. Paisley's writings on his website that no longer exists were excellent on pinpointing the European Union as the final world empire.

The above provide examples of who Jesus referred to when he said he was sending, "wise men." Compare these men with those teaching Bible Prophecy today and there is almost no comparison. Why, because many of the individuals teaching are not sent by God.

6 CUNNINGLY DEVISED FABLES

So many false teachers are teaching cunningly devised fables that they have taken over end time Bible Prophecy news. Many of these are found relaying conspiracy theories. The originator of these are often dubious characters.

Jack Chick of Chick Publications (1926-1998) was a comic book creator and published gospel tracts that sold over 750 million. Jack Chick also embraced conspiracy theories from the Freemasons to Catholic Church conspiracies. He included within his tracts, these conspiracy's for prophetic fulfillment. His source for the Catholic Church conspiracies came from Alberto Rivera, a man claiming to have been a Jesuit priest. This man had a history of fraud from credit card theft to writing bad checks. Through individuals like Chick, conspiracy theories found their way into Evangelical circles. Chick was not a wise man, rather he repeated a cunningly devised fable and helped them become adopted as main teachings in the Evangelical community.

John Birch Society

Robert W. Welch Jr., 1899-1985, a businessman founded the John Birch Society. The society was named after John Birch, an American Baptist missionary and intelligence officer killed by Communist forces in China in 1945. It began as a ultra conservative advocacy group that was anti-communist and promoted limited government. By 1958 chapters existed nationwide. Its influence peaked in the 1970's. Its conspiracy theories dominate the movement. Their magazine *The New American* features articles that promote their theories.

According to Welch "both the US and Soviet governments are controlled by the same conspirators, which include internationalists, greedy bankers and corrupt politicians. The traitors inside the US government would betray the country's sovereignty to the UN for a New World Order or a one world socialist government. In addition, they mark the Council on Foreign Relations and Trilateral Commission as rulers of the conspiracy. Sound familiar? This theory has been circulating since the late 1950's.

No doubt the John Birch Society's conspiracy theories were knowingly or unknowingly adopted by Jack Chic and other Bible Prophecy watchers. Hal Lindsey adopted them along with Pat Robertson. This was evidenced in Robertson's book, *New World Order* published in 1991. To Hal Lindsey's credit, along with citing the conspiracy's he did make mention of the European Community in his book the *Late Great Planet Earth*. He observed that it might possibly be the beginnings of the revived Roman Empire. But he looked no further into the evolving Community. The Maastricht Treaty effective 1993, changed its name to European Union.

The End Time Cults Within the Church

The conspiracy theories and other false teachings have evolved into cults within the Evangelical community. The New World

Order Cult tops the list. A cult is in part defined as a "relatively small group of people having religious beliefs or practices regarded by others as strange or sinister. A misplaced or excessive admiration for a particular person or thing. A person or thing that is popular or fashionable, especially among a particular section of society. In this part of the definition the conspiracy theory itself is what is fashionable.

The New World Order Cult's beliefs are so far out of touch with reality and how the world works, that they fit this classification. The term New World Order has been stretched, abused and misused to fit their end time prophecy conspiracy theory. In addition, the idea of world leaders agreeing in a sinister plan does not happen in real life. Neither do these have any understanding of the functioning of the groups they site It also does not fit the Bible's prediction on how the Antichrist rises to power.

Those who relay the New World Order Cult teachings have no regard for the sanctity of the prophetic writings. In addition, they will not take five minutes to even read how the UN works. They do not value "the sheep" to make any effort to make sure what they teach is accurate.

Finally, as this work shows, these theories have been in circulation for decades. Since the late 1950's. Has it dawned on anyone that not one of their theories have come to pass?

Conspiracy Cults are Anti-Christian

It should be noted that Conspiracy cults are against Christian teachings. They take the view that the conspirators are the embodiment of all evil. Indirectly they are teaching that the Gospel's message of salvation does not apply to them. Neither should any Christian love be extended. Especially in the case with the Freemasons who are viewed as non- human.

Conspiracy's also negate the power of God to work through events. These teachers lend God the help of men: the conspirators. As if God is not able to bring about His own prophetic Word without man's help. Even more it implies the unfolding of prophecy is boring and needs these theories to gain an audience.

Finally, some of the conspiracies are plain vanilla antisemitism derived from the

Protocols of the Elders of Zion and bring anti-Semitism into the Evangelical realm. This diametrically opposes the teachings of Scripture.

Conspiracy Theorists align with a very dark realm. Adherents include White Supremacists and Anti-Semites.

7 THE INTERNET-: SATAN'S DOOR

With the internet, anyone with an interest in Bible Prophecy can build a website. In addition, a camera enables them to upload their commentary on YouTube. Through these individuals Satan has a direct attack on end time Bible Prophecy news. Fables, myths and false teachings now dominate the airwaves.

The Evangelical Community has no standard for those who relay the news. People sitting in their cars telling their visions and lies are considered experts. Christians seeking information are as Jesus described, sheep who are easily led astray. They see "New World Order" or "global government" and other clichés and tune in for more and more disinformation. As they embrace the conspiracy theories and falsehoods, they miss the power of prophecy as its being unfolded through the real order of events.

Search Engines Such as Google-Satan's Feed

Many rely on the search engines to produce the best websites for the information they are seeking.

Under the search for Bible Prophecy within the results are several non-mainstream Bible Prophecy sites. Cults such as Jehovah Witnesses, Seventh Day Adventists and Armstrong dominate the first pages. In addition, the New World Order cult.

Google emphasizes that content is king, but it really isn't. What is a big ranking factor is the number of backlinks, and if content is being continuously uploaded. The authority of a site also ranks a website. Therefore, the Adventists, Jehovah's and Armstrong's are ranking in the top. Their church's with large number of followers give their site more authority and backlinks.

Google Search is not what you think

It is a misconception that Google is the Holy Grail of information. On the contrary, the internet has become too big to get accurate results in any search engine's first pages. Google techs sit around and decide what constitutes a website that should rank. In the process they have killed the recipe by adding too many ingredients. There is a saying that less is more. Google in its early days provided better results than they do today. Unfortunately, the best information that might be available to you is invisible on the internet. These sites can sometimes only be found if you type in entire sentences in search. How accurate is any search when over a billion websites now exist on the internet.

YouTube

YouTube, which is owned by Google operates worse than a website search. YouTube ranks its videos based on the number of views in the shortest time, and how long people stay watching the video. Like Google search, the channels that always making content will rank better. Most new creators will literally become invisible on YouTube.

In the end anyone doing a search for Bible

Prophecy or Bible Prophecy news or updates is getting results that are not what they assume and are skewered. There are many videos making it in the first pages of YouTube only because they continuously produce content. Once I needed to look up one of my past videos, after typing into search all of the information, my video did not show up in any of the pages. With 300 hours of videos uploaded very minute to Youtube, what can one expect?

Google and YouTube are Still Useful

Although Google and YouTube are key instruments for Satan promoting lies, this is not to say they should totally be discarded. You just need to be aware of these facts when you conduct a search. On many searches you are only getting limited information or videos on Bible Prophecy. If you are relying on Google for the best in Bible Prophecy websites and Bible Prophecy news, don't, the results are butchered by Google's SEO requirements. Google, is a leading proponent of AI. Yet with its proclamations of a world soon to be dominated by AI, it repeats the story of the shoemaker who needs to fix the holes in his shoes. Google Search is a mess and often time delivers poor search results. Just be aware and filter through the Bible Prophecy lies it produces. Understand, it is another tool of Satan's to feed you lies.

8 FAKE NEWS IN PROPHECY NEWS

Fake news is rampant on the social networks misleading the public on news events. Shockingly a good portion of it derives on Bible Prophecy news websites. Before fake news became an issue and made the headlines, it existed and was widely accepted in Evangelical Christian prophecy circles.

Paul predicted in 2 Timothy 3:13: "But evil men and imposters will grow worse and worse, deceiving and being deceived." He added in 4:3-4, "For the time will come when they will not endure sound doctrine, but according to their own desires, because they have itching ears, they will heap up for themselves teachers, and they will turn their ears away from the truth, and be turned aside to fables."

I stated earlier and want to repeat again that the word fables in the Greek is from the word mythos. It means an invention, a falsehood, a story. A fiction story: meaning that it is made up. In 1 Timothy 4: 7 Paul's warns, "But refuse profane and old wives' fables, and exercise thyself rather unto godliness."

This is exactly what is being taught by many Bible Prophecy teachers in their analysis of Bible Prophecy and current events. They are teaching lies, and fiction. Especially in the way of conspiracy theories and unfounded, and geopolitically impossible probabilities. In addition, Google and other internet search engines produce in their pages false teachers, represented by their Bible Prophecy news sites. On Google anyone seeking lies can find a steady stream of them.

How to know if a Bible Prophecy news article is fake news

Below is a bulleted list on how to spot fake news from Bible Prophecy sites.

- Investigate the articles against websites that expose fake news' sites.

- If the website focuses on mainly US politics-Republicans vs Democrats-in Prophecy, it is not a reliable site.
- Double check the article in search and makes sure it is written about by major outlets.
- If the site is not a major news's site, be wary of it and double check the about page.
- Examine the sources the website consults and make sure they are top of the line.

Any reference to a conspiracy, click off of it immediately.

9 CRITERIA TO LOOK FOR IN A TEACHER

When you embark on Bible Prophecy news, you need to examine your teacher. Do they fit the wiseman-wisewoman standard? Below is a list of ten criteria, while someone may not fit in all ten, they should fit in most, if not all.

1. **Authored Books**- Are they an author of books? Books indicate expertise. In addition are their books on viable end time topics or some wacky theory.

2. **Scholars- Have they made contributions or added insights into the prophetic forecasts?** Do these individuals provide you greater insights

into the prophetic writings? You do not want to follow anyone who solely relies on other theologians' views or mainstream news headlines.

3. **True Analysts.** Are the teachers you listen to providing true analysis of both Scripture and end time events. Do they point out the Scriptures, they are relating the news too? Do they have a good grasp on the news and provide you background details?

4. **Do they site top of the line news sources for their information or news headlines** Are their sources limited to US media? Do they build their entire analysis or theory based on the latest in the news? If so you are getting a cunningly devised fable.

5. **Are they going behind the scenes?** Do they look at politicians Facebook pages and Twitter accounts? Are they giving you information from press departments? Have they interviewed anyone? These are tasks performed by journalists.

6. **Non conspiracy theorist** If the teacher teaches any conspiracy theory click off

as fast as you can. These have no part in end time Bible Prophecy. They are the core of the lies that are being told. They define as cunningly devised fables and cults.

7. **Personal Background-** As we saw from the Biblical illustrations, we see some correlation from a person's background that sets them up for later entering the kings court. Too often the Evangelical sheep do not require much from their teachers. If a Jewish person living in Israel converts to Christianity, that makes him or her qualified to be a Bible Prophecy expert. Likewise, if they convert from Islamic terrorist groups, that does not quality them to write that the Beast of Revelation is Islamic.

8. **Crossover into King's court** Does this person have any liaison with the governmental political realm? If not, could they be read or accepted by that group?

9. **Correctly Aligned Theology and End Times Views** Does this person's Biblical theology line with the Bible's?

In addition, are their end time views such as on the Rapture, accurate?

10. **Cracker Jack Theories** Is this instructor touting theories that are plain vanilla wing nut material? Such as an alien Jesus or Pax Vaticana? All, which are versions of cunningly devised fables. Are they borrowing from Nostradamus, or of the Last Pope Prophecy of False Prophets? If so stay away.

Below are the automatic disqualifications for any prophecy teacher

- Conspiracy theorist
- Gross errors in facts regarding the European Union, various nations or the workings of international organizations
- Overemphasis on United States politics
- Citing fake news sites in your list of international news's sources
- Grade D or below sources-in the world of journalism. There are grade A sources and every journalist knows these. If a site is reporting Bible Prophecy news it is acting as a news's source and should

hold the same standard of excellence as digital newspapers and magazines.

- Teaching Beast of Revelation or any part of Beast is Islam
- Predicted Mahdi will be the Antichrist
- Literal Babylon view, which identifies Babylon as modern Iraq
- Ephraim and Manasseh are Great Britain and the United States
- United States is Babylon or Beast of Revelation
- Two legs of Daniel identified as Byzantine and Ottoman Empires
- Geopolitical Terms that are dated such as overuse of New World Order
- Cliché Bible Prophecy terms
- Over reliance on US news's sources.
- Copyright violations
- Gross immorality on the part of the teacher

What should a Bible Prophecy News Website or Channel Possess?

A Bible Prophecy news website should hold the same standards as professional journalists and reference top of the line sources, after all it is acting as a news site. The Bible Prophecy teacher should be correct doctrinally and have a scholarly knowledge of the prophetic forecasts. The instructor should also have a good understanding of international affairs. If a site focuses on one area of Bible Prophecy and specializes and does well in that area, it still qualifies for a rating of excellence.

Below. Is a list of good news sources that Bible Prophecy teachers should be consulting.

- News Wires-Associated Press, Reuters, UPI
- Mainstream global media outlets in the EU, US, Israel, Russia, and China. Some have more prestige than others such as the Financial Times over the Wall Street Journal, Euractiv over Politico EU
- Think tanks in both the EU and US and these each have a bias
- Foreign policy journals
- World organization publications
- Central Bank publications, press releases and speeches

- White House Briefing Room
- Knesset Press Releases
- The Kremlin
- The European Commission reports, press releases, audio visual
- The European Parliament reports, press releases, speeches from the MEP's
- Leading university's such as London School of Economics, MIT,
- Interviews with leaders and notables in their fields
- Twitter accounts and Facebook pages of leading politicians
- EU political party president pages, press releases and speeches

The EU news outlets provide EU news and better global coverage than US outlets, which are slanted toward entertaining. You can see this in the varying images of the news casters from this side of the Atlantic to European journalists. In addition, a good deal of news is just omitted because it is not enough to grab the US's viewers' attention. In news, certain publications hold more clout than others. For instance, the Financial Times is read by world leaders. Yet, you never see it as a leading source in Bible Prophecy websites. This proves the inferiority of the sources that are consulted by these so-called teachers.

Five Criteria To Keep in Mind

Below are five criteria to keep in mind as you seek out information on end time Bible Prophecy. In addition, the latest unfolding news.

- Evangelical Christian Doctrine as a basis
- Accuracy of interpretation of prophetic forecasts
- Insight of prophetic passages
- Knowledge of international affairs
- Website Presentation

With all of the above in mind, you should carefully chose what prophecy teacher you will chose to learn under.

10 PAUL'S WARNING

10.Bible Prophecy news is Logical.

The fulfillment of Bible Prophecy in geopolitical realm follows a logical sequence. It is like a puzzle and all the pieces must fit. The parable of the fig tree is a perfect illustration. The trunk leads into big branches that flow into smaller ones. It is a continuous motion.

Bible Prophecy Is Fulfilled Through the World System

Conspiracy's, Freemason takeovers and the like, are just not how the world works. The

Freemasons are a networking group and no more. Bodies like the UN are not a world government, they are institutions that bring together the world's governments into unified positions.

Prophecy will happen through events that are the order of the day. Bible Prophecy news should make geopolitical sense. Look at any of the Biblical prophecies and read the historical events around them.

Concerning the invasion of Babylon in ancient Israel, you can read of the rise of Babylon. On the birth of Jesus and His death during the time of the Roman Empire, you will see that the Roman Empire evolved from the time of Julius Cesar to the time of Cesar Augustus: Rome's first emperor. Why would the final world empire come about any different?

What are you really looking for?

Lastly, you have to examine yourself. Are you looking for entertainment? Do you want your prophecy teacher to relay stories that fill you with fear? Do you want to hear that it can all happen tomorrow? Do you want to be left with so much fear after hearing the teacher that you cannot think clearly afterwards to see that there is no logic to what he or she is saying? Maybe you are not looking for real Bible Prophecy news but entertainment only. You don't want to tune into the fig tree but rather a horror show for entertainment purposes only.

Take Paul's Warning

Many so-called watchmen would not know the fulfillment of Bible Prophecy if it hit them in the face. Take Paul's warning and this book's as well. Search the Scriptures. Examine your teacher. Don't be the one with itching ears. Beware of the wolves. Use common sense. If you are going to call yourself a watchman, don't be one who follows fables and reports them as signs. Rather, search the Scriptures, and do not underestimate our God. He does not need men to fulfill the world of prophecy as conspiracy theories suggest. Prophecy is unfolding just as its written, to the letter. By following the false teacher, you are missing out on prophecy's real fulfillment. Finally, if someone does not provide a correlating Scripture, or cannot back up their geopolitical facts, or if they come out with any shape or form of a conspiracy theory, run.

AFTERWORD

It is tragic that the area of Bible Prophecy news has no standards of excellence that must be adhered to as a prerequisite for teaching. The lack of criteria is almost shocking. Many of the criteria is ignorance based. Literally anyone can come online stand on a soap box and teach end time prophecy. The audience often goes with their emotions and tunes into those having visions or scaring them with the latest conspiracy theory.

Pastors of mega churches who are managing their flocks also rise among the experts, not that they cannot expound on the Biblical piece, but the geopolitical is such an extensive study as pastors they do not have the time required to devote to the topic.

Bible Prophecy news is a serious academic ... Not only must you have a grasp of the ...ecasts, but you must have ... the geopolitical arena and not ... States perspective but a global ...r, you must have analytical ability should be able to add to the teachings instead of relying on what others have written.

Once upon a time I had a Youtube channel called Prophecy Talk, but the appetite for real analysis was so small and the jungle of bad teachers so large who many ran to that I moved onto the secular news arena and left behind daily and weekly reporting of Bible Prophecy news. All of my findings are in my repertoire of my books. Being an eschatologist remains my foundation.

Many of my followers from Prophecy Talk tune into my news show called the Twist. In it I provide commentary from a global perspective with a special focus on the European Union and Israel. Moreover, I am meeting with and interviewing many politicians from different countries of the world and the interviews are on the show. As a strictly Bible Prophecy news teacher you just cannot enter that world without being a journalist or having a comprehensive understanding of world politics. The Twist News is not a step down from Prophecy Talk, but rather a step up. Tune into see why. www.thetwistnews.com

AFTERWORD

ABOUT THE AUTHOR

Erika Grey, author, Bible scholar, commentator, journalist has been a born again Christian for over 40 years She has written numerous books on Bible Prophecy and made contributions in helping to decode the more difficult forecasts. She has spoken on numerous radio stations including Coast to Coast and interviewed high level policy makers.

This book is one of a series of short books by Erika Grey intended to be quick reads with important information. Be sure to check out Erika's other titles at www.erikagrey.com.